EMERGENCY!

HAZMAT TEAMS

DISPOSING OF DANGEROUS MATERIALS

by Justin Petersen

CAPSTONE PRESS
a capstone imprint

Edge Books are published by Capstone Press,
1710 Roe Crest Drive, North Mankato, Minnesota 56003
www.mycapstone.com

LIBRARY OF CONGRESS CATALOGING-IN-PUBLICATION DATA
Cataloging-in-publication information is on file with the Library of Congress.
ISBN 978-1-4914-8029-8 (library binding)
ISBN 978-1-4914-8416-6 (eBook PDF)

EDITORIAL CREDITS
Erin Butler, editor; Nicole Ramsay, designer; Sara Radka, media researcher

PHOTO CREDITS
freetextures: Texture18 cement, 2–32; Newscom.com: Mark & Audrey Gibson
Stock Connection Worldwide, cover, 13, Bart Ah You/ZUMA Press, 5, Tom
Bushey/ZUMA Press, 7, 9, 11, Casey Christie/ZUMA Press, 10, Benjamin
Beytekin/picture alliance/Benjamin Beyt, 14, Bruce Chambers/ZUMA Press,
17, Bill Greenblatt UPI Photo Service, 19, Stan Carroll/ZUMA Press, 21, Ken
Steinhardt/ZUMA Press, 22, Laura Embry/ZUMA Press, 25, Brian Branch
Price/Polaris, 26, Michael Kleinfeld UPI Photo Service, 27, ERproductions Ltd
Blend Images, 29

Printed in the United States of America in Mankato, Minnesota.

TABLE OF CONTENTS

WHEN CHEMICALS REACT

A small crowd is gathered around a burning warehouse. When firefighters notice a strong chemical odor, they called in a unit that handles hazardous materials, known as a **hazmat** team. Four hazmat first responders step out of their vehicle a few minutes later. Every team member is dressed in personal protective equipment, known as PPE. This includes gloves, boots, helmets, hoods, and bright yellow hazmat suits.

The wind changes course and starts to blow harder. A moment later, a hazmat crew member points to the northwest corner of the building. Another fire has started. This one is dangerously close to a chemical facility. Containers full of highly flammable chemicals are stored there.

"Move away from the building!" the supervisor yells into a megaphone. Everyone begins to run. From a distance, the crowd watches and waits. A few seconds later, the entire building explodes. Only a hazmat team can manage this kind of emergency.

Hazmat response units are specially trained to handle incidents involving dangerous substances. The units are often based in local fire departments. These skilled and well-trained professionals bravely risk their own lives to save others.

hazmat–short for "hazardous material"; a material that would be a danger to life or to the environment if released without precautions

Hazmat workers must know how to prepare for many different situations, such as those that may require oxygen tanks.

Chapter 1

TRAINING FOR THE JOB

Hazmat workers train in all areas of emergency response. Training may differ from location to location, depending on the most likely hazards in the area. Many hazmat units require that workers have a background in firefighting or law enforcement. Performing well in these professions requires the ability to think clearly in stressful situations. Hazmat supervisors need to be confident that former police and fire personnel will perform their jobs well under **duress**.

Nearly all hazmat work is done under dangerous conditions. That is simply the nature of the job. Being able to identify a variety of hazardous materials is the most basic qualification. The first thing a technician will do at the site of an incident is **assess** the situation. What is the hazardous material? What is the health risk from this substance? What is the correct level of PPE? Having knowledge of which materials are flammable, unsafe to touch, or toxic to breathe is critical. It can mean the difference between life and death. Hazmat workers complete extensive training to learn how to identify dangerous substances and what to do with them.

duress—the use of force or threats

assess—to judge something's importance, size, or value

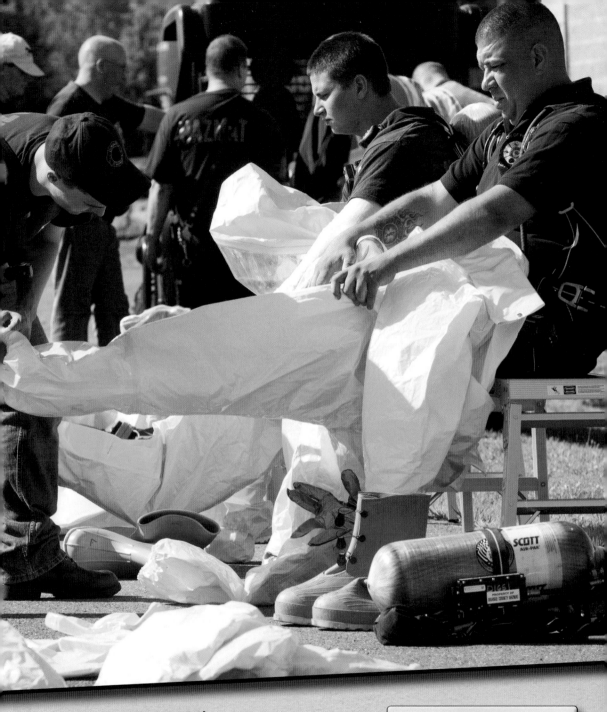

Becoming familiar with the equipment is an important part of hazmat training.

TRAINING COURSES

In order to begin training, hazmat candidates must be in top physical condition. Their bodies need to withstand very hot temperatures inside their PPE. In addition, being in good physical shape makes it safer for them to come into contact with hazardous materials.

Trainees begin by learning the dangers associated with every type of hazardous material. Candidates must then learn to use a variety of high-tech equipment to combat each material. To avoid being exposed to **toxins**, they must become familiar with all types of protective gear. Finally, they learn about the procedures involved with the cleanup, **decontamination**, and disposal of materials.

Depending on the type of hazmat team and the location, specialized courses may be required. For example, the Rail Car Safety course may be a requirement for hazmat teams working near railroads. Terrorism or Weapons of Mass Destruction (WMD) training is a likely requirement for a hazmat technician in a major city.

Upon completion of their training, hazmat specialists receive an Occupational Safety & Health Administration (OSHA) certification. This means they have completed all necessary training to safely work with hazardous materials.

toxin–a poisonous substance produced by a living thing

decontamination–to remove dirty or dangerous substances from a person, thing, or place

Personal Protective Equipment

In addition to the standard hazmat suit, there are many other types of PPE, and each has a specific use.

USES FOR PPE:

- **Respiratory protection—** Responders use respirators to protect against breathing toxic or contaminated air.

- **Eye and face protection—** Goggles and plastic face guards protect against flying fragments, hot sparks, and chemical splashes.

- **Skin protection—** Hoods, booties, and gloves are taped to the hazmat suit so that skin is never exposed to harmful substances.

- **Noise protection—** Earplugs or earmuffs help prevent damage to hearing due to loud noises.

Hazmat workers have help getting into their PPE to ensure that the suits are properly sealed and safe.

Training exercises help prepare hazmat workers for real-life emergencies.

FACT: The term HAZWOPER refers to all training that deals with hazardous waste operations and emergency response.

TRAINING EXERCISES

Training exercises are an important way for a hazmat unit to prepare. "Tabletop" exercises introduce candidates to a variety of hazmat dangers. These exercises are active discussions held around a large table with the trainer directing the topics of conversation. The candidates begin by assessing an incident. They then work together to create an action plan. These exercises allow participants to apply what they've learned without the stress of a real-life incident. There is time for trainees to ask questions and take notes.

In a functional or full-scale exercise, a team of trainees responds to a mock emergency. Hazmat trainers go to great lengths in setting up these fake emergencies. These exercises sometimes involve working with several organizations to safely create a realistic situation. For example, a team of trainees may arrive on the scene of a make-believe oil spill or a dangerous chemical leak. First, they quickly identify the hazardous materials involved. Then they assess the health and safety risks present. The trainees work as a team, carefully putting on their PPE as they develop a plan of action.

Trainees learn how to test their equipment to ensure that it is working properly.

Chapter 2

ON THE SCENE

Radioactive materials begin to leak from a medical shipment in the receiving room at an airport. These dangerous materials need to be contained, or thousands of people will be put at risk. The airport is alerted, and people begin to panic. Minutes later, the local hazmat first responders unit arrives and takes control of the situation. How were they able to get there so fast? How do they prepare to safely contain an incident as soon as they arrive?

First, an airport employee called 911 when he saw a strange liquid oozing from an open container. The container had been labeled with a **radioactive** materials sticker. The transportation of hazardous materials requires this type of warning label, which allows people to quickly identify dangerous substances.

After the airport employee called 911, the local emergency communications center contacted a hazmat team at the local fire department. That team quickly assembled the appropriate PPE for a radioactive leak. They knew exactly what to pack because they had trained for scenarios just like this one. Then they jumped into a specialized hazmat vehicle. This vehicle contained a variety of safety equipment. Many hazmat vehicles, for example, contain mobile laboratories. These allow hazmat workers to test materials on site. They also contain equipment such as ventilation hoods and eye wash stations to deal with accidental exposure.

radioactive–having or producing a powerful and dangerous form of energy called radiation

Hazmat workers approach a scene in full PPE gear, carrying the tools they need.

FACT:
The Ebola virus spread to the United States briefly in 2014. Hospital workers treating Ebola patients wore hazmat suits to protect themselves from contracting the virus.

Hazmat vehicles contain the equipment needed to respond to a hazardous emergency.

FACT:
Hazmat professionals have access to plenty of high-tech gear. Still, the most important weapon in containing an incident is information on the material itself.

PLANNING THE RESPONSE

Once in the vehicle, the senior official begins gathering information. The vehicle is equipped with an incident command center. It includes a two-way radio, a computer, digital cameras, and a digital hazmat library. These hazmat command centers are critical for planning and managing the unit's responses both before and after arrival.

The senior official first calls the person who shipped the hazardous substance to get a complete hazmat Data Sheet. This sheet provides information on all the materials in question, including the container reported to be leaking. The senior official then dials the State Radiation Control Division to report the incident. Finally, she phones the local branch of the Environmental Protection Agency. Her Incident Action Plan, which details her solution, is quickly approved by both parties.

Before exiting the vehicle at the site, all team members meet with Emergency Medical staff. These trained professionals check the **vital signs** of each team member before he or she enters the hazardous environment. They are each checked again after using the vehicle's decontamination shower, and before re-entering the vehicle.

vital signs—a person's pulse rate, blood pressure, heart rate, and temperature; also called vitals

SAFETY ON THE SCENE

After deciding on the response equipment needed, the team members get to work. The first thing they focus on is protecting the people in the area. They **evacuate** the building and the parking lot to within a few hundred yards away. Then they surround the entire area where the spill took place with tape that reads, "CAUTION RADIOACTIVE MATERIALS." This step is critical. Preventing people from coming into contact with hazardous materials is always the top priority.

Every hazmat team member that steps inside the yellow tape is fully protected. They wear the proper PPE needed for the emergency. This includes the full hazmat suit, gloves, booties, goggles, and a hood with a face shield. The suits are sealed off to prevent air getting in or out. Each team member is equipped with a self-contained breathing apparatus (SCBA) that provides clean air. Hazmat suits are also equipped with two-way radios. Team members use them to communicate with one another and with the incident command center inside the vehicle.

Members of the Santa Ana Fire Department's hazmat team dress in the appropriate PPE before entering a scene in Orange County, California.

evacuate–to leave a dangerous place and go somewhere safer

Hazmat Training in Kansas City

In November 1988, six firemen arrived at a reported fire in Kansas City, Missouri. There were two burning pickup trucks parked near an old trailer. These firemen had not been trained as hazmat first responders. They had no idea that 30,000 pounds (13,608 kilograms) of ammonium nitrate were being stored in the nearby trailer. The trailer and trucks exploded, killing all six firemen. This incident led to the formation of the hazardous materials division of the Kansas City Fire Department. Tragedies like these have led to the creation of specially trained hazmat units in nearly every city and

Chapter 3

CLEANUP AND DISPOSAL

After securing the area around a hazardous material spill, the next step is to begin cleanup. If radioactive materials are involved, the entire room needs to be sealed. First, equipment such as heating and air conditioning must be turned off. Then, all of the air vents, windows, and doors are sealed shut using wet towels, plastic sheets, and duct tape. All of this must be done quickly in order to keep the hazardous materials from spreading.

Once the room is sealed, team members clean up the spill using special blue pads. These pads are sponge-like and very **absorbent**. After they have been used to soak up a spill, they are disposed of with great caution.

Sometimes hazardous material spills are **localized**, and only affect a small area. But even when this is the case, team members must be vigilant and check for the presence of chemicals and radioactivity all around the area, even after the spill has been cleaned.

absorbent–able to take in and hold liquid

localized–kept within a limited area

Hazmat workers are trained to deal with leaking containers of toxic substances.

DECONTAMINATION

After a radioactive material or other hazardous chemical is cleaned up, the next step is to decontaminate the area where the chemical spilled. Hazmat technicians understand that even though an area looks safe, it could still be dangerous.

Even after the substance is properly cleaned up, the health risk is still present. For radioactive spills, a hazmat technician might pour a **detergent** called "rad con" over the affected area. But even then, the area may not be completely safe. Radiation can be carried on dust particles. Small dust particles in the air may still be radioactive.

In cases like this, the entire room must be scrubbed clean with detergent. Everything needs to be cleaned, including every chair, ladder, table, floor, and even the walls and ceiling.

Before leaving the scene or removing their PPE, hazmat workers are washed with detergent and water.

detergent–something that cleanses

Hazmat Procedures in Practice

Abby Norman knows how important it is to stay vigilant before, during, and after an emergency. Norman is a hazmat hospital worker in Maine. She is trained to safely handle health emergencies, such as the presence of Ebola in the United States. During training, Norman learned that proper disposal and decontamination of materials is key to staying safe. Because of this, her hospital conducts practice drills every year. Workers practice putting on and taking off the hazmat suit in a way that prevents disease from spreading.

Dangerous materials must be handled carefully and placed into special safety containers before being removed from the scene.

FACT:

Americans generate 1.6 million tons of household hazardous waste per year. Hazardous waste comes from products people use every day, such as batteries, cosmetics, paints, and cleaning products.

DISPOSING OF MATERIALS

To stay safe, all affected materials, including cleaning supplies, must be disposed of properly. Proper disposal of hazardous materials is just as important as containing them. They could interact with other materials and become even more dangerous.

Hazardous materials must be appropriate for the containers in which they are stored and thrown away. For example, certain chemicals, such as **hydrofluoric acid**, can eat through steel containers. Other chemicals may eat through plastic. Some containers will hold radiation and others will not.

After everything is sealed in proper containers, the hazardous materials are taken to a local hazardous-waste disposal site. If the spill was radioactive, the hazmat team must stay on site and continue testing the area for radiation. Once the levels have been deemed safe, they can unseal the area and open it up to the public once more.

hydrofluoric acid—a poisonous acid that is formed by dissolving hydrogen fluoride in water

Chapter 4

HAZMAT IN OUR WORLD

Hazardous materials have been around for hundreds of years. In 1871 the U.S. Congress decided to classify certain materials as dangerous. From that point forward, transporting and disposing of these materials required following basic rules. Over time, rules like labeling hazardous materials and safely disposing of them became more common. Overseeing these rules led to the formation of other important organizations.

By the 1970s, the Occupational Safety and Health Administration had been formed. To this day, this organization oversees hazmat **certifications**. Other organizations, such as the Environmental Protection Agency and the U.S. Department of Transportation, were also formed during the 1970s. Each of these organizations plays a key role in protecting people and the environment from hazardous materials.

certification—an official recognition of a person's abilities and skills

Hazmat workers use Geiger counters to measure radiation levels.

FACT:
The Hazardous Materials Transportation Act was passed in 1975. It improved the laws concerning transporting and illegally dumping toxins that could be dangerous to people or the environment.

Oil spills create a dangerous environment that requires specialized cleanup.

FACT:

BP was responsible for one of the largest oil spills in history when an oil rig exploded in April 2010. The company has set aside $43 billion to cover fines, legal settlements, and cleanup costs.

AN EVOLVING PROFESSION

As people use more and more hazardous materials, more specialized training has been introduced. Special hazmat teams have been assembled to confront some of the biggest dangers of the modern world. The terrorist attacks on September 11, 2001, have had a big influence on hazmat operations. These attacks showed that in the chaos of terrorism, hazardous materials could be present in any attack. Hazmat workers need to be prepared for the unexpected. They may be called in to help other emergency workers in surprising situations. These can include bomb threats or other situations where dangerous materials may be present.

There are also less-scary incidents that occur every day, such as portable toilets spilling off the backs of trucks. Chemical incidents are also common, such as workers at a factory getting exposed to dangerous chemicals. Despite strict regulations, oil spills are a common occurrence. One large recent disaster was the oil spill in the Gulf of Mexico in 2010. During a span of 87 days, more than 200 million gallons of oil were spilled before the leak was contained. Hazmat workers spent more than three years cleaning up the mess.

Some hazmat teams specialize in responding to biological terrorist attacks.

LIVING SAFELY WITH HAZARDOUS MATERIALS

Hazardous materials are all around us. They fuel people's cars. They help construction workers build skyscrapers. They even help produce medicine. Hazmat workers help keep us safe when these dangerous materials are not handled properly. Nearly every fire department in America has a hazmat team. These brave professionals are always ready to use their specialized training to respond to emergencies.

On the scene, hazmat professionals assess situations and identify the dangerous materials present. They then form an action plan and get to work. The world is a safer place because we have trained professionals arriving on the scene of hazmat incidents to contain the danger.

Hazmat workers help keep the public safe from dangerous substances.

Chemical Tragedy in India

One of the worst chemical disasters in world history happened in Bhopal,
India. It occurred early on a December morning in 1984 at a pesticide plant.
A leak caused by a series of mechanical and human failures released a cloud
of lethal chemicals over the sleeping city. More than 2,000 people died
immediately. Another 8,000 died later. Health officials were not informed
about chemicals at the factory. They were completely unprepared for the
tragedy. Since that time, hazmat safety policies have made disasters like

GLOSSARY

absorbent (ab-ZORB-ent)—able to take in and hold liquid

assess (uh-SESS)—to judge something's importance, size, or value

certification (suhr-tuh-fuh-KAY-shun)—an official recognition of a person's abilities and skills

decontamination (dee-kuhn-ta-muh-NAY-shun)—to remove dirty or dangerous substances from a person, thing, or place

detergent (dee-TUHR-gent)—something that cleanses

duress (dyur-ESS)—the use of force or threats

evacuate (i-VA-kyuh-wayt)—to leave a dangerous place and go somewhere safer

hazmat (HAZ-mat)—short for "hazardous material"; a material that would be a danger to life or to the environment if released without precautions

hydrofluoric acid (hye-droh-FLOHR-ic ASS-id)—a poisonous acid that is formed by dissolving hydrogen fluoride in water

localized (LOH-kuh-lized)—kept within a limited area

radioactive (ray-dee-oh-AK-tiv)—having or producing a powerful and dangerous form of energy called radiation

toxin (TOK-sin)—a poisonous substance produced by a living thing

vital signs (VYE-tuhl SINES)—a person's pulse rate, blood pressure, heart rate, and temperature; also called vitals

READ MORE

Harmon, Daniel E. *Jobs in Environmental Cleanup and Emergency Hazmat Response.* New York: Rosen Publishing Group, 2010.

Mara, Will. *Hazmat Removal Worker.* North Mankato, Minn.: Cherry Lake Publishing, 2015.

Ollhoff, Jim. *Hazmat.* Edina, Minn.: Abdo Publishing Company, 2012.

CRITICAL THINKING USING THE COMMON CORE

1. What are some of the common emergencies that require a hazmat response? How are they caused? (Key Ideas and Details)

2. How does personal protective equipment (PPE) keep hazmat workers safe during an emergency? (Key Ideas and Details)

3. Why is it important for hazmat workers to keep learning and training once they have jobs? (Integration of Knowledge and Ideas)

INTERNET SITES

FactHound offers a safe, fun way to find Internet sites related to this book. All of the sites on FactHound have been researched by our staff.

Here's all you do:

Visit *www.facthound.com*

Type in this code: 9781491480298

Check out projects, games and lots more at
www.capstonekids.com

INDEX